Trade Unions:

The Modern Problem and the Christian Response:

Some Suggestions

by

David Attwood

Assistant Curate, Lydiard Millicent and Lydiard Tregoz, Nr. Swindon, Wilts.

GROVE BOOKS

BRAMCOTE   NOTTS.

CONTENTS

ACKNOWLEDGEMENTS

I should like to thank all those who have helped and encouraged me with this booklet, especially those who have read and commented on it in draft. In particular, I owe a number of points of detail to Mr. Robert Hill, and much to the Grove Ethics Group, whose members were unsparing with their time and ideas. Naturally, the responsibility for all that follows is mine alone.

David Attwood

February 1979

First Impression March 1979

ISSN 0305 4241

ISBN 0 905422 53 8

It does not take long in any discussion of industrial events before the familiar battle-cry is raised 'The trade unions are unruly, too powerful, and ought to be curbed'. And, often enough, that is the signal for everyone to bring out his or her favourite anecdotes about union stupidity and awkwardness, of apparently ridiculous restrictive practices, and of inter-union disputes which bring everything to a halt, while the unfortunate hapless managers stand by helplessly. However, such talk as this does not only nothing constructive towards understanding, but it also tends to reinforce the general feeling that trade unions are somehow not really respectable, and that it is not possible to be thoroughly involved in a trade union and at the same time retain one's purity and integrity. My impression (perhaps wrongly) is that many Christians who would question the propriety of trade union involvement would at the same time argue the need and the duty for involvement in, say, politics or business management.

In order to examine the question of trade union membership and participation, there are several issues that need to be tackled. First of all, we need to be clear what sort of an organization a trade union is, how it works, and what its aims are, and to understand the basic dynamics of the situations in which it is involved. Owing to the variety and complexity of the trade union scene, this is bound to be an over-simplified sketch, but it may shed some light on the actual ethical questions that are raised particularly by trade unions and their situation. This section of the booklet will best be illustrated and focussed by various examples. In all this analysis, I will confine myself to Great Britain, as the history and surrounding structures and framework vary considerably in other European countries and in the U.S.A. (not to mention the other two-thirds of the world!).

We must then turn to the question as to whether it is right to be a member of, and actively involved in, a trade union, assuming that this may mean taking industrial action at some time. In other words, involvement means acceptance of collective responsibility for decisions in which one may not have very much influence, and also (and here's the rub) joining in collective action as a result. This raises various questions about moral and theological issues; such as 'Do different moral considerations apply to the collective behaviour of people?' and 'Is a Christian right to compromise with collective bodies which may pay only scant attention to moral issues?' Following on from this, assuming the rightness of involvement in trade union politics, we look at some of the directions in which an ethical stance should lead, by examining a few issues loosely grouped about the notion of justice. It is also important to try to take a wider view, and ask if there are changes which ought to be made to structures, in order that people may more easily live as they ought within them.

Before coming on to these further questions, we turn to a general survey, followed by a brief examination of a few examples.

1. TRADE UNIONS: THE HISTORY AND THE STRUCTURES

The relationship between a trade union and an employer is one without precise parallel. It is partly a power struggle, but it is a thoroughly asymmetrical one. The alleged power of the unions not only varies very considerably from union to union and from industry to industry, but it is in the main a negative power, a power to stop things from being done, not a power to achieve anything without the support and co-operation of others who do actually wield the power. For instance, the part played by Jack Jones in the relatively successful recent period of pay restraint owed more to the personal standing of Mr. Jones, and also to the general agreement by Government, unions, workers, and management, alike that there was an urgent need to bring inflation down, than to the power of trade union leadership. Besides, if it is such, this example of trade union power is probably not the sort most commonly complained of. Now that Mr. Jones' successor, Moss Evans, is leading the reverse campaign to end the incomes policy, it is clear that he and his union could not afford to back the pay policy without asking his members' support and going back on the promises on which he was elected to his position. Whether in fact the unions will succeed in their aim is still unclear at the time of writing (Autumn 1978), but whether they do or not the fact remains that the unions do not actually control the purse-strings, and in this case it is not only their employers but the government also that they have to persuade to let them have the money they are asking for.

Trade unions have arrived where they are as the result of a long, complex and at times extremely bitter history.[1] Combinations of workers were outlawed in 1799 under the Combination Acts of 1799 and 1800, until their repeal in 1824. The growth of combinations, trade clubs, friendly societies and unions continued throughout the nineteenth century, and gradually they won recognition from their employers, who often fought back with imported labour against strikes organized in support of wage-demands.

Union leaders were also liable to prosecution for picketing activities. Gradually unions became less localized, more organized; peaceful picketing was legalized in 1859, and in 1868 the meeting took place which is regarded as the beginning of the T.U.C. In 1871 Parliamentpassed two Acts which partly helped, partly hindered trade unions—their legal position was strengthened, but picketing was again outlawed.

A critical event for the development of the political and legal position of trade unions was the Taff Vale case of 1901, with its aftermath. Very briefly, in this case the House of Lords ruled that union funds could be liable for damages as a reuslt of strike action organized by union officials. The ensuing political events included the appointment of a Royal Commission, and, in the general election of 1906, the return to Parliament of a sizeable pressure group for the T.U.C. (though independent of it), which then took the name 'Labour Party'. After the election, the recommendations of the Royal Commission which advocated a clear legal status for trade

[1] For what follows, I am indebted to Henry Pelling *A History of British Trade Unionism* (Penguin Books, 3rd ed., 1976).

unions, were left aside in favour of legalisation which gave trade unions a kind of legal immunity. This pattern, both legally and politically, has remained substantially unchanged to the present day. There is perhaps one important exception, concerning the relationship between the Labour Party and the trade unions. That is the question whether unions should be allowed to exercise a political levy on their members. When this right was established, the question then became whether or not union members should have to opt out of paying the levy, or opt to pay it (owing to the inertia of members it makes a considerable difference to Labour Party funds which method is used!).

This thumb-nail sketch of the history of trade unions indicates two things. First, that the position of trade unions is very closely bound up with the struggle of party politics in Parliament. Whatever may be the precise position now (are the views of Moss Evans and Sir Keith Joseph really so close together as it sometimes appears?!), this link is very old and deep-rooted. This has the further implication of reinforcing the perceived class differences between employees and employers. (This issue of the class structure in Britain to-day is not one I wish to get involved in, however. But it is indisputable that there is still a strong perception of flses, of 'us and 'them'.) The second point to be made is that the legal position of trade unions as it stands today is one also established a long time ago, dating from times when trade union doubts about the law's impartiality and balanced grasp of industrial issues appeared to be more justified than they are today. Finally, as a comment on the trade union history, it is clear how many issues are very old, and still with us to-day. Take, for instance, picketing, trade union militancy, Government intervention in strikes, not to mention the multitude of Royal Commissions (and how often have they said, as one did which sat from 1891-1894, 'Peaceable relations are, upon the whole, the result of strong and firmly established trade unionism'?[1]). The lesson of history seems to be, above all, that the lesson of history is never learned.

I should like at this point to suggest a cartoon analogy for the relation of trade unions and employers. Although obviously a cartoon, it seems to me that it does have a value and points up some salient points of this ambivalent relation.

The unions are drawn as a lion, and the managers as the lion-tamer. The relation is a mixture of co-operation and conflict—both stand to gain from co-operation. Although the tamer is happy to encourage some conflict, some roars perhaps, his interest is in persuading the lion to co-operate. The lion stands to gain his rewards from the tamer, for his co-operation, but in a different way may also be the winner in a conflict. The show is put on for the benefit of the circus owners and the spectators (the shareholders and the consumers in our cartoon). If the relationship between the lion and the tamer breaks down, one would not at first hold the lion to blame— although it is likely that the lion will appear to be the aggressor. Generally speaking, we would perhaps blame the tamer in the first instance—or the social forces that have put him in this particular job and make certain demands of him.

1 Quoted by Pelling, op. cit., p.121.

What does this cartoon help us to understand? (Obviously it is only a picture, and not to be pressed: perhaps the reader would like to devise amendments—is the T.U.C. more like a carthorse than a lion!?).

In an industrial dispute, things happen quickly, rumours often abound, people in many cases act impulsively. Much depends on what is thought to be the case. Usually it will be the union (or in an unofficial dispute the workers who are protesting) who appear to be taking the first step. This is one end of the scale—where disputes are small and often quickly settled. At the other end of the scale, where long negotiations take place and the conflicting claims and offers do not match up, an occasional trial of strength may take place and a long strike ensue. Here the relationship is much more like that of two people bargaining, or pressing a claim for justice, in a market or in informal legal negotiations. The trade union acts as a balance to the employers' power, and its only weapon is the final one of veto, of withdrawal of labour. In this sense strikes are integral to trade unions, and to join a union is implicitly to accept that a strike may turn out to be the right course of action.

2. WHAT TRADE UNIONS DO

(a) Grunwick[1]

One of the most important disputes of recent years was that at Grunwick, a photographic processing plant in Brent, North London. It is important not only because of the widespread publicity it achieved, but because of the issues raised and the insights gained into industrial conflicts.

This dispute began in late August 1976, at the end of the long hot English summer of that year. Over a period of a week or so, 137 workers, out of a total of 490, walked out of the workplace. These strikers joined APEX[2], and picketed the company right through the winter until the mass pickets organized in June 1977. The mass pickets achieved national notoriety in the media, and caused considerable anxiety and embarrassment to the Government. By this time ACAS[3], who had been involved in working for conciliation virtually from the beginning, had made no progress at all in bringing the company and the strikers together. Legal action against ACAS was taken by the company (following ACAS' recommendation that APEX should be recognized by the Company), which went successively to the High Court, the Appeal Court, and the House of Lords. Before the case was heard, a Court of Inquiry under Lord Scarman was appointed. This took a lot of heat out of the situation—however when the court of Inquiry recommended that all the full-time workers at Grunwick should be re-employed, the company refused—'Never ,in any circumstances will the company reinstate those who were, very properly, dismissed.' In the end, the appeal of ACAS to the House of Lords was dismissed, and their recommendation and those of the Scarman report were of little or no effect. These are the bare bones of a story which aroused great feeling on both sides. On the trade union side the story was that the action was in support of a group who had been dismissed for joining a trade union, in a workplace more at home in the Victorian era than the twentieth century, paying starvation wages to an exploited group of Asian immigrants. On some such basis as this, very considerable time and trouble was taken by trade unionists from all over the country to join the mass picket. On the other hand, the pictures on T.V. that stuck in the mind were, first, the mass picket and a policeman fallen after being hit by a flying bottle, and also the scenes inside the factory when visited by APEX leader Mr. Roy Grantham. This gave the impression that he was attempting to foist union membership on workers who had no wish at all to join.

So, on one side, an intransigent employer who at least heavily dissuaded his employees from joining a union—and on the other, a divided workforce, some who had walked out and subsequently joined APEX and been dismissed by their employer, others who were happy to continue at work on the terms offered by the company.

[1] Much of my knowledge of Grunwick comes from Joe Rogally, *Grunwick* (Penguin Books, 1977). The Scarman report is published by HMSO (Cmnd. 6922, August 1977). The rulings of the Court of Appeal and the House of Lords are contained in the *Weekly Law Reports,* 3 February 1978.

[2] Association of Professional, Executive, Clerical and Computer Staff.

[3] Advisory, Conciliation and Arbitration Service.

We cannot look at all the issues raised by this case. They include the place of the law, its deficiencies and limitations in several areas—the law of pickets, the fact that the law is simply unable to bring or promote trust and goodwill, and mutual understanding. The case also demonstrates the power and the limitations of trade union co-operation and solidarity, and the danger of partial trade union representation, especially where other channels of communication are weak or non-existent. It is perhaps also significant that the workers, who were not well-paid by any standard (starting at around £25-£30 for a 40 hour week in August 1976), were very largely immigrant—and the greatest number of these, East African Asians from Kenya and Uganda. This meant that they had in the main come to England comparatively recently, without much behind them, but at the same time with a good deal of entrepreneurial initiative, and middle-class ambition, (to own their own home, to run their own business, etc.). This combination of economic ambition and starting with very little as a group or community is unusual—one suspects that many other immigrants would be unlikely to organize themselves so quickly or so efficiently, in worse working conditions. The most striking point about Grunwick, however, is not any of these things, the legal position, the position of immigrants, but the gulf that still exists in England between the unions and the employers, and between workers and workers, in small businesses like this. Although, as Mr. Ward (owner-manager of Grunwick) never tires of pointing out, the political establishment tends to be on the side of the unions, at least in what it says, the employer has formidable advantages if he chooses to interpret the situation as one of conflict. And a conflict like that at Grunwick is powerful evidence that Disraeli's two nations, though perhaps not always so easy to see, are still to be united.

We will return to some of the issues of law, and other points raised. But initially it is worth making one or two points about Grunwick itself. First of all, in spite of all the rumour and belief to the contrary, it is not clear that the workers were exploited or badly treated at Grunwick, in comparison with other similar places. Rates of pay were in line with similar processing plants, the working conditions reasonable (although at the time of the dispute the air-conditioning in the place where the dispute started had broken down). Secondly, although it has never been shown that employees were actually forbidden to join a union, union membership was at the least strongly discouraged. In the absence of proper consultative channels, or ways of making grievances known (the mail-order department, where the dispute started, was not represented on the works committee), this was surely likely to lead to trouble of one sort or another. Thirdly, by organizing a partial walkout, the strikers left themselves vulnerable to dismissal—they had no right to claim unfair dismissal when they were all dismissed. Finally, the dispute took on a 'larger-than-life' significance for several reasons. The company was determined to use its legal rights to the full, in defiance of any other view or pressure. Political involvement was there—Cabinet ministers joined the picket line, and on the other side, Grunwick had the aid of a Conservative MP and the organization NAFF.[1] Then the spectacle of violence on the picket line proved grist to the mill for the T.V. cameras.

[1] National Association for Freedom—often considered an extreme right-wing body.

To try to sum up, a number of workers felt they had a grievance, they were angered by the treatment they received and they had no means of expressing it. They walked out, and put their jobs beyond legal protection. Subsequent action by ACAS, the TUC, other unions, the Courts and the Government could do nothing to make their employer reinstate or compensate them. They did not pursue their grievance in the right way, and it is very doubtful whether the trade union movement ought to have tried to force the issue by mass action which inevitably became violent. Although he kept within the law, the employer must also take a large share of the blame. To keep the law is not thereby to fulfil all moral obligations, though it does entitle one to claim protection by the law. It is not at all clear that Mr. Ward is the innocent party, set upon by the roaring lion of the TUC. The cartoon picture suggested earlier needs some amendment here. It would be more accurate to say that one of his team of work-horses had broken loose, and inflicted one or two bruises and minor pieces of damage. The employer-employee relation can all too easily be one of conflict, and in this conflict the employee is likely to need the protection of a union if justice is to be assured.

(b) Some other examples

One of the main tasks of unions is to defend and further their members' interests by representing them in wage negotiations. At times these negotiations break down and a strike or other industrial action takes place to support the claim for higher wages. Roughly half of all the disputes in England are about wages. Altogether, according to Department of Employment statistics, which give a reasonable picture (though this has been challenged) about 2-3,000 strikes take place each year, and about 10,000,000 working days might be lost in a year. This is probably half the time lost through industrial accidents, and a small fraction of that lost through sickness. In other words, strikes are by no means the major reason for English industrial troubles, although strikes and threats of strikes undoubtedly cause more difficulty and disruption of plans than is indicated by figures like these. A proportion of strikes is no doubt caused by greed, and strikes are not always used as a weapon of last resort; but a look at the industries where strikes are common shows that other factors than hasty greed enter the picture. Traditionally miners have had a high strike record[1], though this has changed as mining has become a lot less dangerous and better paid. So too have the motor manufacturing industry, which is notorious for its monotonous, demanding, and unsatisfying, patterns of work, the docks, and the ship-building industry. A significant number of disputes is concerned with parity and differentials.

Striking is only an occasional trade union concern; others include welfare work, and negotiation on issues covering a wide area. One important example is the defence of workers who are disciplined for alleged misconduct. Here the shop steward, the volunteer trade unionist who works on the shop-floor, and normally represents the members of the union at his workplace on a semi-official basis, is involved by virtue of being on-the-spot. The argument may take place suddenly, and it is then the shop

[1] Of course the vast majority of miners' strikes have been unofficial. Richard Hyman, *Strikes* (Fontana, 1972) gives Department of Employment figures for strikes, pp.29-30.

steward's duty to speak and if necessary to act on the union member's behalf. Should the steward by his softness or inaction lose the confidence of his members it is comparatively easy for him to be replaced or passed over. Unofficial disputes can of course take place against his advice or wishes, though he may have little option but to support action against his better judgment, if he feels it is more important to remain a shop steward. Hyman cites a dispute at Ford's Plant at Halewood.[1] It started between a foreman and a small number of men about the way a certain job should be done; the shop steward was drawn into the dispute. After two days, the men stopped work, and there was an incident in which about thirty men were involved and there was an angry scene in the shop manager's office. Although the shop steward, by all accounts, seemed to be calming the dispute rather than stirring it, he was dismissed shortly after. This sparked off a national strike, and the steward was reinstated in a different part of the factory. This incident happened in the context of the firm trying to tighten the formal channels, and clamp down on the unofficial ones operating on the shop-floor, in which the shop steward is the central figure.

Another example of shop stewards' work is that of the four who sued British Leyland for loss of earnings. The case was won by the shop stewards, in a decision given on Monday 9 October 1978, at Cirencester. The firm, in 1972, transferred annual holiday to Christmas, to close the factory for the full Christmas week. This proved unpopular, and in 1974 the management gave an assurance in writing that statutory holidays would only be transferred by mutual agreement between themselves and all the trade unions represented in the plant. But at the end of December 1976, the men were locked out and unable to work. They sued for loss of earnings and were awarded damages and costs. This case is unusual because of the civil action in the courts; however it ought to be noted that, although it was successful, over twenty months elapsed before the case came to court, and even then there was always the possibility of further delay caused by an appeal.

In this case the delay may have caused no particular harm, but it must be remembered that in most cases it it only too easy for management to slow down their response to some claim or grievance and the only method the workers have to demonstrate their concern and get something done is by action to bring home the urgency of feeling. For instance, in the case cited above, at Ford's, the men involved in the immediate cause of the dispute felt that their safety was at stake in what they were asked to do. One might quote here the current (October 78) hospital workers' dispute, whose claim is of four years' standing; whatever its merits and the methods used, their impatience is perhaps understandable.

As a final example of the work done by shop stewards, one might look at a rather different case, but one which points the way to a new and more constructive role. This is the example of the combined committee of shop stewards at Lucas Aerospace. According to a *Guardian* report (19 September 1978) this committee is to be nominated for the 1979 Nobel Peace

[1] *op. cit.*, pp.11ff.

Prize. Lucas Aerospace, the bulk of whose work is used for defence purposes, had plans to make 2,000 workers redundant, but the committee suggested that the factories concerned could be used to make other products of a more constructive nature. Even if the proposals are rejected, it is the right direction for trade unions to look—new and positive attitudes and approaches are needed for today's world, which is not that of fifty, nor even of twenty, years ago.

One way and another, industry in England faces a number of severe crises. By universal assent, it is in a less than healthy state at the moment. On top of that, it faces increased automation, (not least because of such innovations as the silicon chip), and the prospect of more severe competition from overseas. On top of this, no less a person than Roy Jenkins has warned that the car industries must surely be thinking of a complete revolution in the foreseeable future. If the third world is to reach economic viability, this must surely mean increased economic competition for many industries at present the monopoly of the West. In all this, it is surely not only management who have a part to play in the probable adjustments and problems that will have to be faced. By any standard of world history or geography Western Europe has reached conditions of staggering prosperity. But they may not last in quite the form to which we have grown accustomed.

In this situation, the trade unions have at least two jobs to perform. In the first place, it is their task to bargain responsibly and realistically (to use a very tired but nonetheless vital phrase) for their members.

But secondly, unemployment seems to be here to stay. This surely calls for much thought and action to find alternative ways of channelling this available time and energy. Imaginative ways of creating work, not just to help pass the time, but to make and do useful and worthwhile things, will need to be found. In the past, and at the present, the common trade union reaction is merely to defend the jobs of those at work, at almost any cost. Trade unionists can be extraordinarily conservative of the status quo. Here is a really worthwhile cause to be taken up. Trade unions started by working for the poor, the exploited—are they completely removed from those beginnings?

3. A PLEA FOR INVOLVEMENT

Before we come to look at the particular ethical issues raised in our search for a right attitude to, and involvement with, trade unions, there are two basic points which probably solve most of the moral questions faced in practice. First of all, no business, no management, no trade union has a dispensation to break promises, to tell lies, to put matters of so-called 'principle' before the evident welfare of others, to indulge in hatred, bitterness, dishonesty and so on. It is clear that there are many disputes which owe their cause to actions (on either side) which are plainly contrary to any standards of honesty and straight dealing. Now clearly there are disputes which are plain conflicts of interest but many others might not take place—given a bare minimum of concern for the rights and welfare of others, and only a small measure of compassion taken with attention to everyday canons of morality. The second point is that the degree of involvement that a worker takes in union politics will depend on his abilities and on his vocation.

Not everyone is built to be a politician, but all can take an active interest in trade union affairs. As the Lambeth Conference report pointed out 'Christians are not as powerless as they often think'.[1]

All this said, however, there are ethical issues raised in a particularly sharp way by trade unions. Is a Christian right to feel that he ought, in all conscience, to avoid trade union membership? If not, how should he act when called on to support industrial action which he feels is unnecessary or wrong-headed? How should he judge whether a dispute is really justified? Or perhaps, when it is actually unjust and unfair? And finally, given that many disputes may be a matter of virtual indifference, (e.g. a superfluous pay rise which the unions cannot really claim to need or have earned, yet which the management is well able to pay out of profits), how may the trade union be pointed to issues of deeper and much more lasting concern? Is there Christian guidance to what these issues are?

The caricature of trade unions which is widely believed points them as grasping, greedy, dishonest, reactionary, self-seeking, careless of the welfare of others. Furthermore, there is a deeply ingrained feeling amongst some (and not only the higher social strata) that trade unions really ought to know their place, that they have no business to challenge their masters, who are after all the people who have to get things done. A consideration of trade union history, as well as of the immense power possessed by many businesses of to-day, should surely be enough to answer this last (often unspoken but I am sure widely felt) objection. Some trade unions are no doubt closer to the caricature than they ought to be, and some also may seek to use trade unions to further their own political ends. But I do not think the trade union movement is sufficiently monolithic to regard the bad behaviour of a few as a total discrediting of all. Nor is the caricature in many places all that close to the truth. By their very nature, trade unions are virtually bound to get the blame (especially in the mass media) for all industrial disputes, the employers hardly ever.

[1] *The Report of the Lambeth Conference 1978* (CIO, 1978), p.56.

For all that, trade unions do often behave badly. It can be alleged against them that they may stir up envy, greed, and bitterness where it did not exist before, that they create resentment and obstinacy, and that they then support these desires by disruption and conflict where before there was none. They are voluntary associations which do not any longer hold to their roots in early Methodism, but which just make trouble—so it is said —for their own ends.

So the argument for detachment runs. Is not the Christian witness best expressed by standing aside and not being involved?

I think this is a misreading of the situation. Be that as it may, it is much more seriously a misreading of the ethics of the Christian good news. Let us assume for the moment that union membership is voluntary (i.e. that the work-place is not subject to a union membership agreement, a closed shop agreed with the management). Christianity calls people to follow the example of Jesus Christ, who demonstrated a perfect life in thoroughly unconducive surroundings. The Christian is called to live out his life in front of other people, in spite of their weakness and their pressures against good. Jesus himself entered into conflict, he walked into places where he was outnumbered and powerless. At the end, he said nothing, but before that he had argued repeatedly and at length with the authorities. Following him, the Christian is set free from the power of sin and guilt in order to combat its power in his own life, and also to combat evil and injustice in the social order. This he can do by speaking against it where he finds it, by alleviating its effects, and also by seeking ways to put it right at source.[1] In the first place then, the Christian should try to find ways of involving himself in trade union work, rather than just to sit by and watch from the outside. In many places, trade unions are a necessary part of industrial life, and affect all whether members or not.

The Christian is called to make his vision known, and to speak precisely here, where it needs to be seen. Even in places where unions are not so necessary and central, is it not an area of life very much in need of Christian witness and presence?

It may be that it is simply not possible to make an effective protest against what is seen as wrong and unreasonable. Does this deny the Christian's loyalty to Christ, and should he then opt out? First, he needs criteria which will assure him that the trade union is really acting unreasonably,greedily, or whatever.

There are surely many disputes in which it is a case of 'six of one half a dozen of the other'—where there really is not a question of justice involved. It is a question of commercial negotiation and bargaining where harm is not done except in economic terms (we shall look later at disputes where the harm is mainly done to the general public, or some other third party). Secondly, if he is satisfied that the union cause really is unjustified and unjustifiable, he faces the question of whether the issue is one over which he should compromise rather than resign, in the hope that his presence is of value in other ways.

[1] cf. V. A. Demant, *God, Man and Society* (SCM, 1934), pp.21-26.

Here there is not space to go fully into the ethics of compromise. When does compromise just become assent to the status quo, and when is it really a positive approach? How far can the Chritsian go along with much lower moral standards than he would accept in his own life and actions, (and in a trade union a decision often implies corporate action by all)? Evidently this may become a matter of personal judgment about the importance of the particular case and the tactics of the political situation. But there are some who would argue against compromise altogether. Here, I think, there are two points that can helpfully be made.[1]

In the first place, we are called to a severe judgment of our own actions and motives, but a less severe judgment of others. For instance, suppose a shop-steward is the middle-man between a worker and management where the worker appears to be in the wrong, though he has a story, which sounds implausible, to account for himself. For instance, he is being asked to carry out a task but has some objection on unlikely grounds of alleged unsafety. Here the shop steward's task is to believe the man's integrity (perhaps rather as a defence lawyer ought to), where he can, unless he actually knows the man to be clearly in the wrong. The second point to be made about compromise is that group morality is different in some ways from the morality of individuals. Groups cannot be as altruistic as individuals, and the first business of a union is to press for the interests of its own members. In the case of unions there are one or two special considerations. If an official trade union does not accurately represent the feelings of its members, it is at least possible, and in some industries probable, that unofficial action will take place anyway. A trade union depends on its members' support, and shop stewards have only limited powers to act as leaders and tell members what to do. Trade union leadership tends to be delegated rather than representative—it must act according to the expressed views of the membership. (In passing, perhaps it can be noted that it may not be easy for a trade union leader in a public position, with much dealing with Government bodies etc., to remain loyal and faithful to the roots and the people from whom he came. This is perhaps also one of the trade union objections to some forms of industrial democracy—power corrupts!)

To return to our argument for involvement, I have been trying to show that the case for opting out of trade unions membership (assuming that these are substantial voluntary bodies in which there is a real choice between joining and not joining) has to be demonstrated in any particular case; and that this may not be as easy as is often supposed. Membership and support of a body which takes wrong decisions at times is not necessarily a denial of one's loyalty to God. The Christian calling is to be very much involved, as salt, as light. The Christian is to be a peace-maker, he is to point the way to truth and justice, he is to act as a preservative and a saviour in society. If a trade union consistently makes it impossible for him to do these things, then his calling may be to try to show the way from the touchline, but normally the trade union is the place which offers opportunities for witness and action in the first place. To continue the quotation from the Lambeth Conference report:

[1] cf. R. Niebuhr, *Moral Man and Immoral Society* (1933), pp.270-277.

'In some situations only by prayer, suffering and the silent exhibition of a better way, but in others by the resistance and denunciation of evil, by fearless witness to truth, righteousness and freedom by pressure on public opinion and in other ways, it is possible for Christians to help bring about social change, thus acting as the salt and light which Jesus said his followers should be'.

And the bishops go on to point out that this mission must be preceded by our own renewal.[1]

Of course, in many places, the worker does not have the choice of joining a union. Union membership is an explicit obligation of taking the job. Where this is the case, it has become part of the authority structure in a formal established manner. On this subject there is a useful survey of many of the salient points, a Board for Social Responsibility report entitled *Understanding Closed Shops.*[2]

This points out many of the positive sides to the closed shop, although it may under-rate the difficulties that can arise in practice. It points out that the major Christian churches have never taught that association with non-Christians is wrong, and therefore Christians should not avail themselves of the provision for religious objection. It argues that trade unions have done, and still do, much good; and that ethical ambiguity and compromise are at times inevitable. With all this one can agree, and also with the contention that closed shops should be 'constructed with compassion, accommodate diversity' and be 'applied with tolerance'. However, it does not go into any of the theological or ethical issues which underly the problem. It may well be that 'workers who benefit by agreements must join the unions concerned in making them'.[3] But what of those who feel that they suffer more than they benefit from these agreements? Here it may simply be the only way, to accept this suffering for the sake of one's beliefs, and as a witness to one's duty. However there may be another side of it. Depending on what one's duty involves, it may instead right be to regard a closed shop union as part of the authority structure; where, as a result of an authoritative decision, some action or other is enforced on all by the union. Here, in general, one's duty is obedience to the authority, as well as loyalty to one's fellow-workers. The exception here, as anywhere, is that expressed by the apostolic 'We must obey God, rather than men' (Acts 5.29).

There may or may not be the choice of union membership. One way or another, the Christian should approach his union positively, and if he decides to opt out, this surely needs to be argued for. If he cannot opt out, he should view the union as one of the range of institutions to which, within limits, he is subject. But in all this, he needs to have a clear idea of the sort of ideals and aims which he should argue for and throw his weight behind (whatever the level of involvement to which he is called). These fall into two parts. One we may consider as the ethics of coping with the situation, the demands of justice in day-to-day life. The other is the whole range of possibilities for change and reform for which he may catch a vision—some perhaps capable of implementation in the short term, in local situations, others (e.g. involving the law) which are more far-reaching and need much time and energy.

[1] *Report,* p.56.
[2] CIO, 1977.
[3] *op. cit.,* p.13.

4. THE DEMANDS OF JUSTICE

Trade unions grew as a method of bargaining for justice on behalf of the workers who were often low-paid, badly treated. Justice in most cases was very clearly on their side, and in many cases strength on the side of the employers. In these days, the business of trade unions is to bargain for their members; sometimes certainly to make sure that individuals are not treated unjustly by employers, but perhaps more often they act as part of the mechanism of the capitalist market to obtain the best terms for themselves. Nowadays, justice may not dictate which side is in the right, any more than justice tells us the fair price for a packet of tea. (It may be that the consumers exploit the producers if the price falls below a certain level, or *vice versa* if the price is too high—but generally this will leave a range in which other factors operate).

What I propose to do is to examine five areas in which the concept of justice may be thought to apply—pay, industrial action, the public (or the consumer), and the worker's life both as employee and union member. I shall use two working criteria to try to identify an unjust action:

(1)   any action is likely to be unjust if it breaches agreements or promises, or agreed procedures, and

(2)   any action is unjust which shows a disregard for the rights and welfare of any individuals affected. Clearly these are not the only possible criteria, but they will serve as a guide, to help pin down 'justice' rather more closely.

(a) Parity, anomalies and justice

The question of parity is one of the most common causes of anger, and one which often leads to prolonged difficulties. Skilled people worry because they fear, not that they are not paid enough to live comfortably, but that they are not paid more than those doing unskilled work. The shipbuilding and the car industries, with their wide ranges of skilled and semi-skilled crafts and trades, are fruitful areas for disputes. To take a recent example from elsewhere—surely it is not right that those who supervise work in hospitals should be paid less than those whom they supervise? We can probably all multiply examples of difficulty and dispute. Is it then a just cause, for instance, to seek parity between people doing the same sort of work in different places, or different factories?

Certainly on the face of it it looks as if it ought to be.

Without wanting to go into this subject in detail, it does raise a number of questions, such as: should we try to plan together a kind of national pay structure which attempts to find agreed scales, or should we let the market find the levels for us? Is it possible to do the former, or is it the latter course which will lead to great unfairness? Would planning and interference cause more problems than they would solve? How are we going to face the increasing strains of apparently ever-accelerating technological advances? Are some who are fortunate and control the capital resources (either, perhaps, owners or labour-forces) going to be increasingly richer, while others live on what they are given? Whether these or others are the right questions, it does not seem that we have begun to find sensible and helpful approaches to them yet.

But perhaps one may put a question-mark against the whole rigmarole. Basically it is this. Almost everyone in the West now earns enough to live fairly comfortably, and in Britain those who don't are assisted by the state. To argue about whether, if I am earning £75 per week, and my neighbour is earning £80, that is fair or not, seems quite unreasonable, granted the enormous disparity between such sums and those available to people in desperate need elsewhere. Neither of our criteria for injustice apply here, and if we are to talk of 'comparative injustice' we ought to broaden our field of comparisons.

What worries people in these positions however is not the precise figure, but the comparison. The worrying thing about the comparison is that we have a tendency to feel that 'we are paid what we are worth'. Therefore, if someone else doing the same as I am receives more for it, what worries me is not simply envy at his extra £5, but that I feel he is more valued than I am. This is no sooner stated than it appears ridiculous—for in fact people do not rate others as they are paid, at least according to the social surveyors —but nevertheless the ambiguous language of the question 'How much is he worth?' gives the game away. We do tend to rate individuals according to the money they earn. This tends to bring much added anxiety and energy to questions of parity, anomalies, and differentials, an addition which is surely genuine but also misplaced.

(b) Unjust union action
Just as employers can behave badly, so too can unions. There are several areas in which it seems that unions can behave badly and unjustly.

(i) Action that is taken which is clearly out of proportion to the grievance. (I do not wish to include here action against consumers, who are in no way party to the dispute, but injured victims of it). What I have in mind is action which entails huge disruption which is out of proportion to the wrong that is to be put right. Normally however this tends to happen only when the small grievance is a symptom of something much deeper—for instance the problem may be not merely sympathy with one dismissed employee, but anger at the whole tone of employer-employee relations. Nevertheless, unions can be tempted to use their strength to gain concessions in an unfair way—for instance, threatening disruption when the employer is working to a deadline, or seasonally very busy. When this is done without due negotiations and procedures, it is an unethical and unjust method of bargaining.

(ii) Action which breaks existing agreements and procedures. It seems to be all too common practice for employers to delay and to stall over wage and other demands; nevertheless unions ought to stick to agreements and promises that they have made. Workers ought to abide by union decisions. I would not wish to condemn unofficial strikes as such, for, given the unofficial nature and workings of many trade unions, strikes often start (with union approval) as unofficial, and then are made official after a few days. But sometimes they are not, and then they should be called off. There are also sometimes disputes which are 'unofficial-unofficial'—i.e. not approved of formally by the union, nor informally by the shop steward on the floor. These, surely, cannot be justified.

17

(iii) Political demonstrations. Sometimes government employees strike to force the government to pay them more, but other strikes against the government are surely inappropriate. The trade union movement has a particularly powerful political lobby and should use this to work for political changes.

(c) Justice and the employee

Reference has already been made to the work of unions in helping to ensure fair treatment for individual employees who are disciplined, or badly treated by employers in various ways—bad working conditions, for example, and a variety of other possible causes of friction.

It is often in this sort of circumstance, when a union has a complaint or grievance to which it is felt there is no effective response by the management, that sudden unofficial action on the shopfloor forces the employer to take action. It seems to me impossible to say that such action must always be wrong—any more than one could say that it is always justified. If there is a genuine cause, and the employer is stalling in the hope that it will fade in time, one can sympathize with those taking action. At the same time, such a procedure as this is also clearly open to abuse.

This question raises one of the central issues of modern industrial work. Who should control the work, how it is done, how fast it is done and so on? Who is in charge of the working environment, who should have control, those who own the plant, those who manage and organize its use, or those who actually have to do the work? The relation of the worker to his work was analysed by Marx, who wrote:

> 'that the work is external to the worker, that it is not a part of his nature, that consequently he does not fulfil himself in his work but denies himself, has a feeling of misery, not of well-being, does not develop freely a physical and mental energy, but is physically exhausted and mentally debased. The worker therefore feels himself at home only during his leisure, whereas at work he feels homeless . . .'.[1]

This is part of Marx's analysis of alienation, and although perhaps things have changed in some respects in 135 years, in other respects Marx's analysis of the working situation still carries conviction. Control of one's working situation is an important part of being able to enjoy the job, and this debate is often a basic feature of many modern industrial disputes. It is in this light that 'restrictive practices' should be viewed, for instance.

It is surely in this context that one should put the current anxiety about mechanization, the loss of jobs; surely the paramount issues are not the economics of the decisions, but the wishes and opportunities open to those directly involved? For instance, it may be sensible to allow a man near retirement to continue to do work (even though it could be done by a machine) but short-sighted to insist that young people are trained to do the same job.

[1] Economic and Philosophical Manuscripts 1844; to be found in *Karl Marx: Selected Writings in Sociology and Social Philosophy*, ed. T. B. Bottomore and M. Rubel (Penguin Books, 1963) p.177.

All this discussion goes to show that 'justice' in this context is not a concept which is easy to pin down, let alone identify in practice. In the first place, some of the procedures which are in use are cumbersome, and insufficient agreement and understanding exists for them to be effective. But secondly, although it is clear that ethical issues, of right and wrong, of justice and injustice, are involved, there is insufficient recognition that these are significant questions, and insufficient agreement (for everyone tends to use these words as slogans to support his own cause). In this situation, there is a need for more discussion of these issues, and we will come on to definite suggestions in the next chapter.

(d) Justice and the consumer

In our increasingly interdependent social and economic life, a dispute between a small group of employees and their employer can have extremely widespread effects on a wide range of people. Those who appear to have great importance feel their bargaining power is greater than those whose work has not the same central character. Yet this power often falls quite arbitrarily—compare the results of an all-out strike by social workers as against prison warders. Who would have thought that the country could so easily withstand a long fireman's strike, with apparently comparatively little loss of life or even economic damage. Yet we are constantly discovering small groups of workers who have the power to bring essential services virtually to a halt—take the petrol tanker drivers or the hospital supervisors. Some distinctions may easily be made. Some who strike only deprive other people of other things, (car workers for instance, yet a spanner thrown in the works at one place can bring the whole machine to a grinding halt). At the other end of the scale, some have, paradoxically, so much power that they can virtually never actually use it. The firemen, for instance, did not prevent the army from saving life, and indeed in many cases helped where they could. The police are not allowed to strike, and a few other vital forces (the services), but this is a sanction that has to be compensated for. There was a great deal of condemnation recently for the hospital supervisors, over what appeared to be a comparatively trivial though long-standing complaint, who may have greatly increased the risk to life for some in need of hospital treatment. There is fairly widespread agreement that industrial action should not put life at risk, and that if it does, the Government has a duty to take action, and thereby break the strike if necessary. This is a starting-point which could be built on.

There are many groups of people who can only take industrial action by affecting those with whom they can have no quarrel. One thinks of such groups as teachers, social workers, prison officers, hospital workers, whose work is for the direct benefit of a limited group of (often needy) people for whom they are caring in a direct way. Social workers and teachers are perhaps examples of those with comparatively little industrial muscle, whereas those in prisons and hospitals may have a fairly direct and critical effect by strike action. Perhaps one can only plead for a sense of perspective amongst such workers, and also ask that those responsible for their pay, working conditions, etc. do not take advantage of their goodwill and sense of vocation. Surely action taken by people in these areas which can only affect others in no way responsible must be in desperation. Even recognizing that it takes two to make a dispute, one must question whether ingenuity could not devise other forms of action which demonstrate the frustration without hurting those who are already in need of some sort.

(e) Justice and the union member

Unions vary enormously in their strength, their ways of working, their militancy, and their general approach. But they all depend for their strength on the unity of their members, and in particular their power to dissuade or prevent blackleg workers from strike-breaking. It is also true that the results of union action are then available to all members, whether they contributed to union effort or not. This clearly is bound to cause resentment among those who may have made considerable personal effort or sacrifice to support the union. Loyalty to one's fellows in this situation is no evil, but there may be circumstances in which the individual feels there is a higher call on his conscience. Provided that the union action is taken properly and democratically, this loyalty is surely not normally to be outweighed by loyalty to the employer. In this case, the loyalty (and this is recognized by most employers) must be to the union first. This of course underlines the need for trade union democracy to work fairly, properly and effectively —though this also depends on the employers' attitude.

But the union can make too much of the loyalty it claims from its members, either by action which is itself unjust to the individual, or when it attempts to prevent him carrying out some higher duty (such as caring for the sick, the needy) or asks him to put other lives at risk.

First, some unions have great power over individuals. In particular some trades are controlled by unions which operate a 'pre-entry closed shop', where a worker has to join the union before he can be employed. There have been unhappy cases, too, where men who have held sincere objections to trade unions have lost their jobs when a trade union has become a closed shop. There is a range of government and quasi-legal machinery which can be appealed to in the case of unfair exercise of union power. The Board of Social Responsibility report comments cautiously about this: 'There is here potentially effective machinery for dealing with problem cases in actual closed-shop practice'.[1]

An injustice which may be harder to prevent occurs when individuals are locally victimized for not taking part in industrial action. There have been reports, for instance, of firemen who refused to go on strike being very badly treated after the strike. Whatever one may feel about the strike itself, and those who refused to take part in it, surely both employers and the official unions have a responsibility to all to ensure that victimization does not take place in such cases, and if necessary to take adequate practical steps to overcome it. One accepts that it may not be wholly preventable, but to stand by and watch is surely not justifiable.

Some unions are powerful, and individuals need protection from abuse of that power. It is not clear whether that protection is always available, but it seems to me a matter of some concern that it should be.

[1] *op. cit.,* p.5

In conclusion, our survey of these five areas may seem rather inconclusive. The word 'justice' does not always have a ready, straightforward application. What is important is to examine the whole context, to try to understand the underlying structure and forces operating.

One then needs to ask about what is really happening, to see what is important from a Christian perspective. (Is the size of the wage packet so crucial to man's proper self-esteem? Is the closing down for a few days of a range of factories as big a disaster or threat as the media would have us believe? Does modern industrial work sometimes rob man of his dignity and humanity?). Within this framework, we then have two questions to point out injustice:

Are individuals being very badly treated by the actions of others? and Is some agreement or promise being broken?

The questions then raised are what constitutes bad treatment, and whether the agreements are really agreements, well-known and recognized by all.

5. SOME POINTERS FOR THE WAY FORWARD

We have already seen that there are substantial questions that need to be asked about everyday assumptions which are made about work, wages, industrial power and so on. There are a number of large areas that there is not space to go into in detail. It would be interesting to make a comparison between Christian and Marxist views of work, its context, and its effects on man. Following from this, it would be worth exploring differing attitudes to conflict in the workplace. All we have room for are one or two comments on this. There is always potential for conflict, but it is by no means always necessary or desirable. Certainly there are postures taken up by both sides, and old customs retained from the past which emphasize the conflict, not in a merely ritual but in a thoroughly substantial manner. Where trust and understanding are so vital, it is surprising that so often so little attention is paid to them.

(It has been noted that relations between officers and men in the contemporary Army are both more relaxed and more effective than those between management and workers in modern industry!) Union customs, for their part, often embody old attitudes and suspicions. Sometime with good reason, but often not, trade unions cling on to old victories and agreements which are no longer relevant or beneficial to their members. In some respects they can be the most conservative bodies imaginable!

Here there is plenty of room for Christians to catch a vision for new ways forward. Another such area is that of Industrial democracy.[1] One of the problems of industrial democracy is that it is difficult to make provision adequately for the expression of conflict between the two sides. We have already seen that one of the risks from the union point of view is that representatives elected to the management side may not remain loyal to the wishes of the workers. But some of the difficulties may also arise from a general unwillingness to make changes. Workers ought not only to be able, but to be encouraged, to have a say in the way their work is done, and the uses to which it is put (I do not mean products taken 'on the side'). This applies right the way down from board-room level to the shop-floor. In some ways industrial machinery dictates the terms on which it has to be used. Yet surely the struggle must be for the worker not to be enslaved by the machinery, but for him to be master of it as far as possible. In this context, surely experiments which give variety and meaning to boring production-line tasks should be encouraged, and unions should be amongst those pressing for such experiments and possible improvements. It is a positive gain if men are more satisfied and fulfilled in the work that they do (even if this leads to a possible loss of union power owing to a lower level of discontent and militancy).

In short, trade unions need a new vision, and also to be entrusted with a much more positive role in order to begin to put such a vision into practice. Their first task is still to defend their members' interests; but they do operate the basis of democratic structures (albeit in need of overhaul and reform in

1 The reception of the Bullock report has been very disappointing. *(Report of the Committee of Inquiry on Industrial Democracy,* Cmdn. 6706, HMSO 1977).

some respects) which could be of great positive value. To do this they need to operate in an atmosphere of greater trust and co-operation. In a sense, the initiative has to come from management—whose first task, which is so often seen as the making of money at the cost of all other considerations, should include the security and fulfilment of workers in their jobs.

Legal Reform?
The law has now a long tradition in this country of refusing to involve itself in trade disputes.

The recent attempt, in the Industrial Relations Act, to bring trade unions more clearly within the ambit of a defined legal framework, failed largely because of lack of trade union co-operation but also because most employers are very unwilling to use legal pressure—it makes more trouble than it is worth. There are other difficulties in legislating for trade unions and disputes. One major difficulty is that it is very hard to legislate to decide on the issue at stake—one can only legislate for the procedures to be followed in pursuit of a dispute. This means that the legal issue is likely to hang on technicalities (such as whether 'notice' is given in the correct way, or whether a strike is a 'breach' or 'suspension' of employment).[1] The other major difficulty lies in the question of enforcing civil liability on unions. Unions are not rich, in comparison with the sums of money which may be alleged to be in jeopardy in a large dispute. Further, if the strike is unofficial, and the union is not involved, it is hard to see how liability can be enforced. To exact penalties on a few leaders is more likely to create martyrs than to deter others—the sanction is simply ineffective.

Nevertheless, it is not clear that the present arrangements are sufficient, even allowing for the limitations of the law in dealing with trade disputes. We have already asked if there is sufficient protection available in law for individuals who are wrongly treated by trade unions. It is not clear (following especially from the Grunwick case) whether ACAS has sufficient legal backing. But it is clear that legislation affecting unions can only be made and become effective where there is a consensus of union opinion to support it. The atmosphere generated by the Industrial Relations Act is surely sufficient demonstration of this.

We have also seen that some distinctions which at first sight appear to be clear and simple are not so—e.g. the distinction between official and unofficial strikes. Union structures are by no means simple—in particular the Donovan Commission concluded that there are 'two systems of industrial relations. The one is the formal system embodied in the official institutions. The other is the informal system created by the actual behaviour of trade unions and employers' associations, of managers, shop stewards and workers.'[2] There is a number of other complications which have not been mentioned so far. There is a wide range of industrial action available to unions as well as actual strikes—works-to-rule, overtime bans,

[1] cf. Maurice Kay, 'Strikes: Law and Community Interests' in *Perspectives on Strikes*, ed. Ronald H. Preston (S.C.M., 1975). I have found much else of value in this symposium.
[2] Quoted by Pelling, *op. cit.*, p.266.

refusals to do certain duties or to operate certain machinery. Another complicated area varying enormously from factory to factory and industry to industry is that of inter-union disputes and rivalries. How can these be made amenable to legal judgments?

Even if some of these complexities could be brought into the scope of the law, the law itself would do little to improve relations. What suggests itself is the need for greater articulation of what constitutes 'good industrial relations practice', and a strong general willingness to promote it and abide by it. Particular industries have done this in many ways, in the form of jointly agreed documents, codes, etc. ACAS has to date published three codes of practice[1], which attempt to clarify certain matters without actually having the force of law. No doubt more will be issued[2], and if they receive general acceptance they could help greatly to provide a framework which is agreed to be the norm.

Other areas are further removed from the reach of the law and both formal and informal codes. Industrial action itself is very little affected by such, except for the general respect for life which keeps emergency services going. In two ways it ought to be possible to go further than this. Firstly, industrial action should be a last resort, and not entered in haste and anger as it so often is. Secondly, those whose strikes hurt, not their employers, but clients who are already in need, have an obligation to find other tactics wherever they possibly can. There is room for moral judgments, but not made ignorantly or censoriously.

The urgent call is for Christians to take courage to think and speak positively. Their vision for the future can include such things as these: that a man's worth is not to be measured by his weekly take-home pay; that it is an abuse of strength to use it at the expense of the weak; that unions must look to the interests of others, such as the unemployed and the really poor, especially in the third world. In detail and in practice there is much to be done. Trade unions need much creative energy to perceive and work out a new vision for justice and general welfare, to come to terms with new challenges and to respond positively. In their involvement in the power structure, unions are in danger of losing the moral impulses which had much to do with their early rise. They cannot go back, and should not try to, but for the future they need a thoroughly wakened and articulate mora, conscience.

---

[1] e.g. Code of Practice 3, *Time off for trade union duties and activities* (HMSO, 1977).
[2] An obvious candidate for a code of practice is picketing; issues of particular current concern, such as secondary picketing, and others, could be tackled in this way.